The 2 Keys for Highly Exceptional Teams

~ LEO SIMPSON II ~

Copyright © 2019 Leo Simpson II
All rights reserved.
ISBN: 9781711526539

Dedication

To my good friend, Dylan Sorge.

From our $3,000 value conversations has come the inspiration to enrich the lives of others with the concepts and perspectives that are transforming our lives and the way we influence business success.

THE 2 KEYS FOR HIGHLY EXCEPTIONAL TEAMS

~ Table of Contents ~

Foreword 5

Chapter 1 – Discovery 8

Chapter 2 – Getting Granular 14

Chapter 3 – Why Keys 18

Chapter 4 – Gap Bridger 21

Chapter 5 – The First & Greatest Key 25

Chapter 6 – The Second & Equally Great Key 31

Chapter 7 – Using the Keys 1.0 38

Chapter 8 – Using the Keys 2.0 48

Chapter 9 – Rise & Fall 54

#TheExtraMILEwithLeo 60

Make A Difference 61

#BeTheRealYou 62

Book Leo 63

Foreword

When I first met Mr. Leo Simpson II approximately 5 years ago, I only knew him as an acquaintance and family friend. However, over the last year and a half, I've grown to know him more intimately as both a mentor and a brother. The impact he's had on my life in such a short time speaks volumes to the knowledge and passion that he possesses when it comes to enriching the lives of others.

When he first asked me to write the foreword for this book, I was a little surprised as to why he asked me. I knew he was aware of my keen ability to write and communicate effectively (which are skills I thought I could no longer utilize until he helped me reinvigorate those talents), but writing a foreword for a book is something I'm completely unfamiliar with. Although, once he explained why he selected me, I didn't hesitate for the opportunity because it was a reminder as to all that he has instilled in me over the course of the last year or so.

So why me, you may ask yourself? By society's standards, I'm a nobody. I don't have some glamorous career, or drive a fancy car. Neither do I travel to luxurious places once a month and just "live it up". In fact, currently, my life is quite the opposite. I'm 30 years old. I live at home with my parents. I work a contract job earning only a couple thousand dollars a month, and also due to my own foolish behavior in my early twenties, I have significant health issues that most traditional medical doctors don't even know how to handle. In fact, if you looked up the term "hit rock bottom," you'd see the story of my life, up until this point, listed as an example.

However, connecting with Leo was the glimmer of hope my life needed. My eldest sister suggested that I reach out to him, and upon our very first chat, he suggested that I take a course he created called the "Be The Real You E-Course," and that day was one of the best diagnoses that I've ever received in my life. Through completing the course and also by consistently meeting with Leo, he deposited some major keys in my life for how to move forward.

One of the main lessons that still stick with me is understanding how to maximize your unfulfilled potential despite your circumstances, and I certainly do have circumstances. Another, is the belief that I'm not a prisoner of my circumstances and that I have a lot to offer as both a leader and consultant in the areas I wish to pursue professionally.

Thanks to Leo, I now have clear cut plans on what I want from life, and despite how long it may take me to reach those goals due to circumstance, I understand that for the first time ever, nothing is stopping me. And the power in believing and knowing that for a guy like myself is both lifesaving and reassuring!

So I write this to say how I'm 100% confident this book will help you and others grow in the areas of leadership and team building. Perhaps some of you reading this may not even think of yourself as a leader with vast potential, like I once did, up until Leo gave me the tools to dream again and understand that it's never too late to become a better version of yourself. So please, do yourself a favor and allow this book to transform your mindset into someone who doesn't just survive the workplace or life for that matter, but thrives!

Chike Ogbonna
Aspiring Culinary Artist
Mentee & Brother of Leo Simpson II

Chapter 1
Discovery

Have you ever looked up, aha moment, to see if it was in the dictionary? If you said, No, I'm in the same boat with you. However, I did search the statement one time to make sure that I spelled, aha, correctly and I observed something very intriguing. Aha moment is actually in some dictionaries, and of its number of definitions, one refers to it actually meaning discovery. Now why do I bring up discovery?

I once read a quote by Albert Szent-Gyorgyi which says, "Discovery consists of seeing what everybody has seen, and thinking what nobody has thought." How many people have seen the statement, aha moment, and never really looked into the depth of it? I was one of those people for a while but like this quote, I happened to see things the same way others do and thought a little differently than most have.

I bring this up because that is at the heart of what took place in the discovery of the keys that will be discussed in this book. For me, I was not looking for these keys. I was not looking to develop a concept associated with these keys. I was just going about my day to day and somehow they begin to emerge. There was my aha moment!

So what am I talking about?

Well, in the day to day engagements with my daughters, ages 9 and 4 at the time of this writing, the very scope of these keys began to emerge. What I mean is that as I focused commitment that was necessary in my engagement with them, these keys became very clear. It's easy for me to have just went about my day to day with them and not function in such a way that the value I gleaned could be extracted and leveraged, but because I tend to think a little differently than most and have a sense of absorption of circumstances to glean things that seem to be unique, I could not help but to see these keys blaring and staring at me.

So I had to look into them and I'm glad I did as they have served: me well personally, my daughters well, my engagement with my wife well, my professional influence on business optimization well, and team excellence very well. This discovery that I had has become such a profound reality that the businesses and teams that have begun using it have not just seen profound results but they have seen things that can be described as "You can't make this stuff up."

What are you looking for from this content? Are you looking for discovery? Are you looking for discovery that will level up your team for the purpose of leveling up your organization? Are you looking for perspective that will cause your team to hone into its focus and capability as well as its strategy in order to produce the highest level of excellence?

Are you looking to discover a golden nugget that becomes something that changes everything for your financial future? Are you looking for the answer for why your team is not being what it's capable of being or in other words, really tapping into its potential?

Are all of these questions your questions or just one of your questions? Regardless, you are in the right place to engage in discovery, and in the words of Marcel Proust, "The only real voyage of discovery consists not in seeking new landscapes but in having new eyes."

It was not where I was that made the difference in this discovery. It was the way in which I looked at where I was and what was happening that affected this discovery. If you should take the time throughout this short read to allow your eyes to be opened in a way that they have never been opened before you will see things that you have only imagined could emerge within the scope of your understanding and clarity.

What I want you to know is that there is an unlimited amount of potential available for you to tap into. There is, in other words, an abundant adventure that awaits you in discovery for the purpose of being able to be excellent, effective, efficient, encompassing, and exceptional. The aim here in this book is to not just give you something to discover but to inspire your discovery. Why is that important to inspire your discovery?

Well, inspiration leads to enrichment and when enrichment exist, the produce of that enrichment has a major impact on the potential to be exceptional. The thing that we should ask though is what is inspiration and what is enrichment? I think it's important to ask these as well as answer them briefly in this section because they are at the root of discovery. So let's break these down a little bit and then take you, a little further with the rest of the book.

Let's first look at, what is inspiration? Look at many dictionaries and you'll find something very similar across all of them that emerges as a common denominator. You find that inspiration deals with breathing into. The example I like to use with regard to inspiration is CPR, also known as cardiopulmonary resuscitation. What's unique about CPR is that the person who is receiving it in many instances is not breathing.

Not all the time is the person who is not breathing able to be resuscitated but in many instances they are. The inspiration part is facilitated by the person who is performing the mouth to mouth procedure in the execution of CPR. What this person is doing is breathing into the body of the other person. That is, the person who is unconscious or not breathing is having breath breathed into them. They are being inspired.

What happens if the person being inspired doesn't respond to the inspiration? They don't discover life again. It may be something beyond the control of that person that affects their ability to awaken and respond to the inspiration. However, let's assume that the person being inspired has the ability to respond to the inspiration and if they choose not to see the inspiration as something of value and benefit to them they will remain where they are without life and breath. So, inspiration is key because it and its effect give the ability for new life to be discovered for there to be value and, watch this, an enrichment that may follow for that individual who has been inspired. Now let's look at enrichment real quick.

If you do the same thing that was done with inspiration with the word enrichment, you also find something that was very common across all definitions and that is that enrichment simply means betterment. Is it fair to say that, using the example of CPR for someone who is unconscious and not breathing, by responding to inspiration and awakening from its effect lies a significant amount of enrichment? I think everyone would agree with this.

The reason for agreement is there is a significant amount of betterment that exist in breath returning to a person after being unconscious and not being able to breathe because the appreciation for life after that experience is so much more serious. It's hard not to see the full scope of benefit of being able to breathe.

What I believe you will experience here is what I experienced in bringing this content to you – Discovery. Make no mistake about it, you have done more than just purchase an intriguing book. You have done more than just make an effort to advance your team. You have done more than seek for solution to establish a solid focus and construct for the achievement of results in your business. You have done more than just be a learner. You have exhibited a hunger and desire for inspiration that you may be enriched with true value for your life contribution and achievement to be exceptional.

Let me tell you, something special happened to me in this discovery that is about to be shared and in the discovery of the need to share it with the world. My hope is that your discovery is as profound and greater than that which I have experienced. Let me lead you into the remainder of this book and your discovery so that all that is exceptional can emerge for you.

Chapter 2
Getting Granular

I actually have a secret to tell you. Before I tell you that secret, I want you to have a good awareness of the word, granular. Granular speaks to getting down to the grainy level of the little details. We live in such a fast-paced environment, society, and generation. As a result of this reality, getting granular is not really important for many. But can we afford not to get granular? Can we afford not to get down to the nitty-gritty? Not if you want to be exceptional.

So here's the secret. There can be no exceptional teams without exceptional people.

Now you may look at that statement and say, "That's not really a secret!" I see where you are coming from. However, as it relates to this book and its content, just think about it. How can we say, highly exceptional teams without really speaking of highly exceptional people? We can't.

To illustrate what I'm thinking, I share with you my experience not too long ago where I had the opportunity to look into the story of Dr. J – Julius

Irving. As I watched the story of Dr. J and his progression from the projects to the playground, and from the playground to the professionals, I saw something special. I saw Dr. J as a mesmerizing player and entertainer. I also saw Dr. J as a winner. While Dr. J never stopped being mesmerizing and entertaining, when he began to play in the NBA being a winner began to be questioned.

Dr. J was initially a player in the ABA before the ABA and the NBA merged. Dr. J was someone special in the ABA league. He single handedly brought a new flavor, a new fire, and a fresh energy to it. He took the stage with the sense of accountability for being the chief representative of exceptional results and achievement. That wasn't the case immediately when he became part of the NBA following the merge. Don't get me a wrong, Dr. J was exceptional, but his team was not exceptional enough to win a championship.

Interestingly, he was a mentor to Magic Johnson when Magic was considering to leave college early and enter the league. Then Magic Johnson became a thorn in his flesh for the attainment of the ultimate goal of becoming a champion in the NBA. Dr. J was an exceptional player but his team was not an exceptional team. In other words, there were not enough exceptional people on the team with Dr. J for them to be exceptional and achieve an exceptional goal.

From this thought is where I encourage you to think as you progress through this book. Think about it, Dr. J was an exceptional player but his team wasn't an exceptional team. They went to finals after finals after finals. No championship for Dr. J. Then it seemed that something magical happened. Moses Malone is brought on the scene in 1983. Then what do you know? Dr. J finally wins a championship. What happened? Why, with the addition of just one guy, did the whole dynamic change? Truth be told, it is very simple.

The Philadelphia 76ers had not yet assigned to their roster the right players in order to create the right result. In other words, they had not positioned themselves to become a highly exceptional team because they had not yet acquired the right combination of people with the right potential to become highly exceptional people who then influence the team to become a highly exceptional team. Getting granular about the scope of a team or better yet getting granular about who and what makes up a team is more important than the result of the team itself.

The team is a unit of multiple people working in tandem with one another based on the right focus, perspective, and concepts. What you must understand is that for a highly exceptional team to emerge related to the keys which are about to be discussed shortly, it is really important that these keys be valued, benefited, and cherished by people who can become highly exceptional rather than just by teams who want to become highly exceptional.

It is important that we remember that a team is the surface of the core which are the people. Show me a people who are not committed to what it takes to be exceptional people and I will show you a team who only dreams of being exceptional but never being able to truly free that dream into reality. Show me a team with people who are committed to what it takes to be exceptional and I will show you a team capable of tapping into their potential without restraint or reservation.

We are getting much closer to talking about the keys that must be committed to for a team to become a highly exceptional team. There are, though, some thoughts that we need to address related to the keys in general so that we can be clear on the value of the two keys once they are revealed. So let's jump into why we're talking about keys.

Chapter 3
Why Keys

There are many influencers who have written on various topics relating to achievement of teams, employees, managers, leaders, and other groups or roles. For example, Stephen Covey is well known for talking about habits of highly effective people. John Maxwell is well known for talking about laws of leadership, laws of growth, and laws of teamwork. There are others who have used different concepts or terms to describe their specific content that are critical in producing achievement, results, value, and success. However, after much thought I choose keys. Why keys? I think you might have some indication of why but let me tell you a story about some wisdom my dad shared with me to convey why.

In my last semester of undergrad at Grambling State University, which was in 2006, I found myself in a position where I became burnt out. I had extracurricular activities that were very engaging. I had classes that were demanding because they were the last of my curriculum. There were graduation requirements. I was a resident assistant.

By this time in my college tenure, you can say that I was an important guy on campus with some important roles. I think the biggest thing was that it was the last stretch. I was a runner in high school and the last stretch of a race was always the toughest for me. To be honest, it was the stretch where races were really won but I never really executed during that time of the race to really see the results that were truly possible for me except for a few times.

So, here I am in my last semester and I call my dad. I call him with tears in my eyes and a somber voice. On the other line he's, I guess you could say, sympathetic. After I tell him how I was feeling and what I was thinking, he says to me, "Brother man, you are at the end." What I said to him that caused him to say these words to me was, "I feel like quitting." You can imagine how I felt on the other end to hear those words and be reassured that I could finish. Not only was he saying I could finish, he was saying that I had to finish. What would have been the point in being at Grambling State University all the way through to my last semester and saying, "That's it, I'm done with this?" Would have made no sense.

Moreover, in the context of this conversation with my dad and the profound statement above, he said something else that was so wise. As a matter fact, he had shared this with my brother me on numerous occasions prior to college. He said to me, "The degree you are about to get is a key." He says so much more but the point of what he said was that my perseverance to attain and complete my degree would provide me with the key that, even if I didn't use it, could be used to open doors that I would not have the ability to open without it.

You see, I could follow suit of Dr. Covey and say the two habits of highly exceptional teams. Or I could follow suit of Dr. John C. Maxwell and say the two laws of highly exceptional teams. While I revere these influencers and others like them, I would not be true to the discovery. The discovery I made revealed keys.

Yes, these keys may influence habits. Yes, these keys may be influenced by laws. What you need to know is that, though they are in some way affected by habits, laws, and other terms, these keys will enable you to unlock things, access things, and command things that habits and laws cannot. There are some things that just need keys for them to be accessed.

Why keys? What if you tried getting into your car, turning it on, and attempting to operate it without a key? What would be the point of that? So, as it relates to people becoming highly exceptional and in doing so influencing the becoming of a highly exceptional team, how important are your keys? They're very important. Let's briefly talk about one critical reason why they are important so that we can take our dive into the keys.

Chapter 4
Gap Bridger

Remember we talked about how keys are critical for the access of doors which have things behind the doors. The two keys that we're going to be talking about are even more critical and valuable to understand clearly and explicitly because of the mentality of the current generations. Right now we live in a time where millennials (of which I am one) are becoming the leading professionals as the Gen Xers are transitioning out and the iGeners are replacing the millennials on the front lines. One thing about the younger millennials particularly and the iGeners is that there are some fundamental awarenesses that many of them have not engaged work wise because of certain pleasures, exposures, and luxuries.

Regardless of this being the case, it is important for those who will be leading these groups and coming after them to be very clear about the two keys about to be discussed. Unfortunately, it is no longer the case that these two keys and their accompanying wisdom are inherent and being exhibited holistically in our economic environment.

To be honest, many are oblivious to these keys, which by the way are really simple, and are limiting their ability to excel and achieve exceptionally because of not having a clarity or knowledge about them. As a whole, there is the reality of us being confined to an illusion.

Have you ever heard the quote by Daniel Boorsten, "The greatest enemy of knowledge is not ignorance but the illusion of knowledge?" Whether, Yes or No, here's why this quote comes to mind. I believe I said to you earlier that you know the two keys (if I didn't say it, I surely thought it). You know each word that makes up the keys.

You just don't know which words they are and why they are of importance. The danger in this is that while these terms are known independent of one another but not in their combined state and representation as keys, there is the pursuit of achievement and results with a value for having information rather than a value for implementation and execution.

I would like to share with you that since I have been sharing these two keys with business leaders and owners, executives, and operational level people, I have seen the light bulb go off for them. One situation in particular was when a gentleman, who happens to be a millennial, not only dramatically increased his productivity but has become more valuable and has noted that he is committed to growing and developing in ways he had never considered. What's even more profound is that this reality in his life has bridged the gap between ownership, leadership and management, and himself as well as with other members of his team.

These two keys are like a most beautiful bridge well placed between the current generations and those who will come after them. These two keys are like a beautiful bridge built between vision and operation. These two keys are a bridge from potential to potential. These two keys are a bridge between wisdom and application. These two keys are a bridge between dreams of teams and their realities.

Just think about the most beautiful bridges in the world or even the not so beautiful bridges. What would it be like if those bridges didn't exist? How much more difficult would it be for us to cross from one side to the other without the bridge? How much would not having the bridge impair us from achieving the things that were possible? Don't get me wrong, I know that there are those who would find away, but this is a small minority.

The two keys we are about to discuss are just that important. They not only bridge the gap between generations, ideas, vision, wisdom, and so many other things. These two keys shake something inside of every person who gets them and enables them to engage and unleash a fire within them that they had no awareness existed.

I'm not telling you what somebody told me. I'm telling you what I know. What you are about to hear is so absolutely simple but you may not have ever heard it put this way. So, as I discovered before, I now reveal the two keys and share with you in your discovery for becoming a highly exceptional person who influences highly exceptional teams.

Chapter 5
The First & Greatest Key

I have played on a number of sports teams over the course of my life. I found that every team I was part of had one thing in common – a vision. Every team wanted to go somewhere. Every team wanted to accomplish something special. Every team wanted to win. Every team wanted to be exceptional. However, just because every team wanted the things aforementioned, it doesn't mean that these things were going to become a reality.

There's something more that is needed for the vision and the desire to be manifested. It is easy to see what is good in our mind and have an eagerness for it to appear in reality, but the gap between the two is very real and there is something needed in order to close that gap so that there can be the presence of exceptional achievement and growth.

I shared with you all earlier in this book that my discovery of the two keys came as a result of my engagement with my daughters. More specifically, my discovery came when my oldest daughter was our only child. I was doing a pretty good job raising her in collaboration with my wife but was missing something, and I didn't know what it was. What ended up happening was a brother-in-law of mine approached me and asked if we could have a conversation about some things he was observing in how I was engaging my daughter. This lead to various awarenesses related to my engagement with my daughter.

Let me tell you, many of the things that were shared with me in that conversation I knew but I didn't know them in the way that it was presented; I had the case of an illusion of knowledge and it was very clear to my brother-in-law in his observations. It is often times in our life that we know something but because of it not being constructed in such a way that we are able to leverage it and that is most profitable, we either lose or barely win. That was the case for me. I had an awesome vision for my daughter. I wanted to see that vision manifest into reality but I was missing something very critical. As a result of me missing something critical, my daughter was also missing something critical.

My daughter's first name starts with a G and due to the fact that my wife and I have a duty to prepare her for life, that makes us part of Team G. What must be understood is that if we fail to do our part now as it relates to her long term success and achievement, we will not only lose in our leadership effectiveness, she will lose in her ability to excel most efficiently at critical points in her life. What am I getting to? I'm getting to the key.

In order for Team G to be exceptional, the people who are part of Team G must be exceptional. So what is it that is going to help the people of Team G be exceptional in order for Team G to be exceptional? Remember I told you that you know what these two keys are, you just don't know that they are keys? Well now it is time to unveil the first and greatest key. To unveil the first and greatest key, let me tell you a story from my years in middle school playing basketball.

I was most skilled as a shooter and a defender. I was also very good at assists and at free throws though I did not get to shoot free throws much for being reluctant to drive to the basket. When it came to shooting, I was good at mid and long range jumpers but for whatever reason, the coach that I had made me feel like I didn't know how to shoot or, for any matter, play basketball.

I could be wide open after a number of passes and he would holler out from the sidelines, "Don't you shoot that ball." How counterproductive to putting points on the scoreboard? There would be other times where I would do exactly what he wanted me to do and then be taken out of the game. I didn't know whether I was coming or going, riding the bench or playing in the game.

I didn't know what I was supposed to do even though I knew how to play basketball.

Most often, beside believing that my coach was nuts, my thought was, "What does he want from me?" Here's the thing, what is it that both my coach and me along with my teammates were not clear on? We were not clear on expectation. That's right, the first and greatest key for highly exceptional teams is expectation.

Why is expectation such a critical key?

Let's look at the example I just gave above regarding the engagement between my coach and me. I thought I was on the team and in the game to play basketball and help win games. However, it seemed like everything that I and everyone else would do was contrary to his expectation. It's almost like I should have interviewed him before I started to play basketball to determine if I was going to be able to be clear on what the goal was and how we were going to get there just to play middle school basketball.

I just don't see how you can tell people don't shoot the ball when they are wide-open and expect to win games especially knowing that the person who is wide open can shoot the ball really well. Now, in all fairness my coach really wasn't a bad guy. He was strange and I'll tell him that to this day, but he wasn't a bad guy. I just believe there was a fundamental error and miscommunication in regard to expectation.

On the other side of the athletic spectrum of basketball when I was in middle school was another coach for a different grade level. This coach not only made clear his expectations but it was obvious that his players knew exactly what the expectation was. I mean, his team would blow other teams out of the water.

They made us look like we had no business even thinking about basketball. Not to mention, when we played the same schools, the outcome was the polar opposite and the difference in the results they were getting versus what we were getting was not talent or skill set. The difference was simply expectation.

On the one hand, I have seen that having a clarity of the importance of expectation has changed the trajectory of my daughter's life in an extremely positive way. Mind you, this is not just the case for my oldest daughter I spoke of but also my youngest daughter.

My point is that my wife and I take very calculated and intentional steps in working to ensure that the expectations for our children's life is clear. We know if they understand clearly what is expected of them they will be more equipped in leveraging the second key which is equally great.

On the other hand, I have seen how taking this key along with its counterpart key into the professional environment is able to transform the productivity of an individual and their team dramatically. I witnessed a professional go from saying, "I'm not going to change or do anything different than what I'm doing," to saying, "Wow, I have been wasting time and putting energy where it does not belong." I assure you, when expectations are clear it is almost guaranteed that delivery upon them will be profound and value will be exceptional. So, what's the second and equally great key?

Chapter 6
The Second & Equally Great Key

This key is one of my favorite keys. I don't mean it's one of my favorite keys of these two keys. If that was the case I would say that this is my favorite key. There are keys for other things in life. There are keys of growth. There are keys to leadership. There are keys to success. There are keys to friendship and relationship. In other words, there are keys to unlock other doors in life. This one is one of my favorite. As a matter of fact, I think that these two together are my favorites.

This key in particular is one that is used in various different ways but is specific in every way. What I understand about this key, what it really means, and how powerful it is only became clear about a year ago for me. I heard this word many a times throughout my life. I heard it in relation to so many different applications of my life. It never was so clear than when I heard Richard Pimentel share his story about it.

Richard was in the military – Vietnam War veteran. While he was in Vietnam, there was an experience where he had to put his life on the line to save the lives of other soldiers. He tells the story of how his leader asked him to do something that was very difficult to give life to others, and it was the perfect synopsis of the key I had ever heard. Let me jump to the part in his story that gets to that synopsis.

In his story, he tells of a situation where airborne support was unable to get to them. From airborne support came a call that communicated that reality with a contingency solution. The solution was that a side of the hill could be blown up to allow soldiers to escape down the other side. The catch was that there would need to be someone to hold off the enemy so that the escaping soldiers don't get flanked. Richard tells the story of when the call comes in and how he responds with, "And who might that be?" His leader then says, "Richard, we have to do this."

Richard is appalled. He expresses it, too. His leader then says to him that they have to do it, with a follow up question of rebuttal from Richard of "Why?" His leader says, "Because it's our responsibility." Before we go on, let me take a quick moment to say that you have just witnessed the second key – responsibility. I told you that you knew both of these keys. Also, I told you that you probably would not think that they were the keys associated with this concept. That's one of the beautiful things about mindset inspiration. I digress.

Richard's leader continues and asks if he understands or knows what responsibility it is. It's then made clear that responsibility is the combination of two words – response and ability. What is shared with Richard is that it's important to look at this situation from the standpoint that there is an ability that exists to respond to this situation, and because the ability exist then there should be a response appropriate to that ability. Richard, his leader, and others responded with their ability to hold off the enemy and helped a number of soldiers escape without being destroyed or captured.

Let's talk real briefly about what makes responsibility so powerful and one of my favorites.

There is a Bible story that is known by the title in some translations, The Parable of the Talents, or in other translations, The Parable of the Servants. In this Bible story it speaks about a master who has three servants. What this master does is assemble before him his servants in order to give to his servants of his substance prior to him going on a journey. One of the most interesting parts about this story as it is written in the biblical text is that the master gives to his servants according to their ability. Did you catch that? The servants receive consistent with their ability (to respond).

After the master gives the talents to the servants, he goes on his journey and we see something intriguing. We see that two of the servants respond with their ability immediately and produce a return on what has been given to them. Then we see the other servant use his ability in a unique way that is quite opposite of the other two servants; he takes what has been given to him and buries it.

The day comes when the master returns and all of the servants come before him. The first servant that received five presents to the master five more than he received. That servant is commended and given the invitation to enter into the pleasure and joy of the master. The second servant has an identical experience after having taken the two that he received and getting two more. The same could not be said for the last. The one who had received one comes before the master and delivers an elaborate speech to explain why he had nothing more to give than what he had received. After giving his spill he makes his presentation by giving back to his master what his master gave to him.

It's possible that you might be looking at this and thinking, "How insane," or "This dude was crazy!" I would agree with you. Now, I certainly would not have seen myself as that guy but there was a point in my life where I was and maybe so are you. Let's dive a little deeper into what is happening with this servant.

Remember I said earlier that the master gave to each of the servants consistent with the ability he knew they had. That means that the master knew that the inherent ability would also make possible response. Therefore, there was an expectation that each one of them consider their ability and then respond appropriately with their ability.

In full observation of the story at this point, the master speaks out and does not commend this servant but actually condemns him. Now, many Bible scholars and believers of the Bible deal with the aspect of the servant's wickedness, slothfulness, and laziness which are all true. I want you to hone in, like a hawk, on something interesting and a little different. When this master speaks in condemnation to this servant, he said something specific. Let me quote for you the text as it is written so we can see the same thing together. It reads,

> "But his master answered him, 'You wicked and slothful servant! You knew that I reap where I have not sown and gather where I scattered no seed? Then you ought to have invested my money with the bankers, and at my coming I should have received what was my own with interest." (Matthew 25:26-27, English Standard Bible)

When you look closely you notice something unique in the master's words, "You knew…" What is the master saying here? He is saying the expectation was clear.

The problem was not with the master as the servant's elaborate excuse attempted to assert. The problem was not in the expectation not being given or being unclear. The problem was that the servant failed to respond with his ability consistent with the expectation. Don't miss this. This servant responded with his ability but he did not respond with his ability consistent with the expectation.

When I saw this in this story, I was fully convicted of my mediocrity and the level of averaged living that I had engaged. As you engage with the content that I write and author, you'll learn a lot more about me especially as it relates to how much of a quitter I was. That's not what this book is about. I only want to bring this out because I want you to know that I was like this servant. I was responding in life with my ability but inconsistent with the ability I had to deliver upon the appropriate expectations. As a result, I affected the outcomes of a number of teams.

One experience in particular that I will briefly share was when I quit the cross-country team going into my senior year in high school. Yes, going into my senior year, I decided I wasn't going to run in the sport I had participated in for 3 years and would have been a second-year varsity team member. How foolish was that? Fate would have it that they would make it to the state finals that year, place in the top 10, but not win. Just think if I had been there responding with my ability consistent with my potential in its unlimited capacity. What could have been the result?

Without this key, the first has no true substance. So, as we get into the application of these two keys being put into the doors to unlock highly exceptional reality for people and teams, realize that they are independent yet dependent. It's kind of like having a dream. If you have a dream but no action to free the dream into reality, the dream is just ideas and thoughts in your head.

On the other side, if you have actions to free a dream into reality but no dream to be freed, you're nuts. You need both to be combined and in tandem operation. When they, expectation and responsibility, operate together there is the emergence of something that is exceptional in people and teams that make a significant difference in the environment around them.

Let's move on to give you some substance on how to make use of these keys and draw on the value and benefit that they offer.

Chapter 7
Using the Keys 1.0

Everyone has a unique set of abilities that they are able to respond with. The problem comes when ability is not responded with due to there being a lack of clarity in expectation. To elaborate a little on the perspective shared in the chapter on bridging the gap, I want to provide some insight into this idea that I've just mentioned so that there is a sense and awareness of the power and purpose of these keys.

One of the things about the generation of leaders and workers transitioning in and those coming up behind them, is an overabundance of entertainment engagement. I don't know if you have noticed, but when people are highly engaged in entertainment at the degree that many of the younger millennials and especially the iGeners are, there tends to be a significant lack in the area of focus and excellence. Now do not get this confused or twisted with there being a lack of ability. It is simply a display of focus and excellence being limited. Why is this?

Due to the fact that when being entertained – a.k.a. being detained for entry – there's no need to really think, rationalize, engage, or get involved in depth, what is mainly going on is that the one being entertained is being engaged by that which they are being entertained by. There is no skill set being exerted by them. There is no reasoning faculty being challenged or perfected. There's an extreme amount of disengagement on their side and an extreme amount of engagement on the other side. However, the side that the disengagement is on is with those who need to skillfully engage in order to produce results in their endeavors and efforts for their benefit and the progression of society.

The difficulty has emerged to engage people in things that don't entertain them and that they are capable of excelling in but have little willingness to focus on because they have been highly entertained. Entertainment has its place but it is not designed to replace engaging people at the level of expectation and responsibility in a practical, continual, exercised manner. It can pretty much be said that the execution muscles related to expectation and responsibility to produce excellence and sustainable results have gone unattended, undealt with, and undeveloped.

What we must understand is that the primary labor force that will influence our economic progress in the very near future and the foreseeable future are these people who have not been exercised, worked out, or well prepared within the scope of expectation and responsibility. In many ways, they are like newborn babies trying to play in a professional league that they should be ready to integrate into. With these two keys and the mindset behind them having not been emphasized, the effectiveness and efficiency that they bring have not been leveraged best as they would were they clearly communicated.

While completing my master's degree in Executive Leadership, I worked part time for Target. It just so happened that, during that time, I was working at a location that was participating in the piloting of a change management process.

I had a very unique seat of observation having had experience in management and currently working on my master's degree while in my role with Target. I was able to see the change management process with so much clarity and effectiveness because of being free to take in the information and perspective, process and use it in my studies, and then apply it in the operations.

It was kind of like I was a manager being able to work and test the strategy without reservation. If you've ever been a manager in a change management process, you know that one of the challenging pieces is having to give the information and influence others to execute it without being able to know for yourself if it really works. I, again, just happened to be in a very privileged position having been a manager but not being in a management role and being able to use my management experience and expertise in the execution of the strategy.

When people needed to be trained, I was the go-to trainer and considered to be one of the best trainers.

Even after three months of being in my role, I was honored as team member of the month. I was somebody who could be counted on. If not careful, you may think that I'm tooting my own horn. Not so.

I'm sharing these things for the purpose of setting up the keys and how to use them effectively. I told you I will give you practical examples of them at work. Fortunately, I have been able to apply these keys myself to know they work for me before they have been shared with others.

What was it that caused me to be associated with the things I just mentioned? I think you know what I'm about to say. It was expectation and responsibility. In what way though?

If you were a guest or a team member at Target and asked me what my role was, I would say, "To influence amazing guest experiences and drive awesome sales." Period. That's not what they told me to say though what they said inspired what I began to say (and do). Regardless, what they communicated to me set my expectation and the clarity of it. I was committed to respond with my ability at the highest level possible to deliver upon that expectation.

Therefore, my commitment was to be an amazing influence on guest experience so that the sales would not just be okay or good but awesome. I wanted guest to love their experience when they walked into our store. As a matter fact, they wanted to love their experience and know that their presence was appreciated when they walked into our store. I know because I asked.

One particular guest shared with me that the manner in which I engaged her was not only very much appreciated, but that she believed it to be important in making the experiences of all of the guest profound. This particular guest was basically saying that guest expect a certain type of experience, and when they experienced it, they would respond with their ability in how they shopped and purchased in the store.

Let me take you a little deeper because this guest was touching on something. There was more to why I wanted to influence amazing guest experiences and drive awesome sales at the core of my expectation and responsibility. It was the awareness that when people spent their dollars in our store, they were spending something that was much more valuable than just the dollars. What were they exchanging?

Think about this. Our store had about an average basket size per day of approximately $40. If you know anything about retail, you know that there are some serious transactions. I mean you have people spending hundreds of dollars at a time. To have average of $40 actually said that we had a lot of small transactions that are probably somewhere in the ballpark of the 50s, 60s, and maybe even 70s as well as a number of them being well into the hundreds.

You've heard the saying before that "Time is money," right? Well it is not true. Sure, money and time can be measured together but they are not equal to each other. Saying, "Time is money," is like saying that time is equal to money (time = money). That's not true because time is actually greater than money (time > money). So, then what is it that is actually equal to money? Life. Yes, time equals life (time = life).

With this in mind, let's just say that a guest who comes into Target earns an average of $20 an hour. If the average basket size is $40 dollars, then that means that people are spending two hours worth of the time they spent earning income in the store. Even deeper than that, they are spending dollars associated with life they gave away to their work to receive it. Naturally, it would make sense that guests expected exceptional value when they came into the store to spend their money.

I cared that the guest had an expectation and a responsibility, and depending on how I delivered upon that expectation with my responsibility would determine how they would then engage their responsibility. In layman's terms, the guest wanted the greatest value possible in order to give us their money. I wanted them to give us their money but in order for me to influence them to give us their money, I needed to make sure that I gave them something that their money was worth giving to. So, I would give them the most amazing experience possible so that they could spend the most money they were willing to spend and impact awesome sales. I enjoyed every bit of it.

Here's another application example from a different environment. There was a point that I worked with

UPS. I worked with UPS as a seasonal driver, a part-time pre-loader, a full-time driver, and a supervisor for on road personnel. As a supervisor for on road personnel, there was a huge operations management opportunity in the business center that I was assigned to.

To be honest, there was a huge leadership and management opportunity and it was evidenced by these words when I arrived, "Our center is the worst in the free world." That was the description of the business center and its function at the time that I arrived. That meant that in all of UPS International, we were at the bottom.

Let me tell you, this is no sob story. I was the last needed piece of the puzzle for our operations management team. We all brought different skill sets and years of experiences, and when we found our groove, there was no stopping us. I was the youngest of the management team in terms of years with the company and in the operation, but I brought a unique energy and insight that added great value to the exceptional managers that I was around (think Dr. J & Moses Malone). What I brought most of all was the awareness of expectation and responsibility.

I oversaw on a regular basis a driver group of about 15+ driver service providers, but on any given day I could actually be overseeing the full breadth of the service providers up to 75 or more. One of the things that my business manager was able to lean on from my skill set and perspective was the delivery on clear expectation and the influence of taking responsibility. We did not use the terms expectation and responsibility explicitly but the keys were there.

Every morning we started with what are the expectations that are being set for us for the day by virtue of what we have to work with and how are we going to respond with our ability. What do we have at our disposal? This was every day among the management group though it for sure extended to the operational personnel. When it came to engaging them, especially when they didn't have the most ideal situation for the day, we always had to remind them of the expectation regardless of the non-preferred reality.

There would be times that I would have drivers come to me and say, "Leo, take a look at my truck; how am I going to have a day that is going to be most ideal with this?" I started responding to them with, "You're the master, that's your beast, now go tame it." They would look at me funny initially and then shake their head, get in her vehicle, and do what they had to do. In other words, they would respond with their ability and deliver upon the expectation of taming, in this case, their wild beast of a route for the day.

In moments like these and others, all I was simply doing was reminding our team that ultimately there was an expectation for them to do one thing, be a driver service provider. Their job was not to determine if their route was most ideal. Their job was to take the situation they were given, use their skill sets and experience to service our customers. The point was for them to know and commit to the expectations, then take responsibility.

Now, I wasn't just the perspective guy, I was also the energy guy. I could energize you with perspective and excitement. During our peak season, the business managers of our division along with our division manager came up with a saying to share with all driver groups to influence perspective for the day throughout the peak season.

When it was shared with our management team, I got excited. The reason I got excited is because I saw how I could use the saying to level up what we were already doing to improve our operation. The first day they let me lead the group in the saying, the building rang with roaring voices and energy from our team of about 100. People began coming from different directions in the building to see what was going on in our business center.

Here's what the saying was:
No late air
No missed pieces
We service our air
We service our customers
And when we come to the intersections
We look left, right, left

It is outside of the scope of this book to give detail on what all of this means, but these things stated our priority expectations for our drivers. Being able to have these expectations in such a clearly defined manner but also in a way that could be energizing was priceless to me.

So, I would get on our platform as if I was speaking to a crowd of thousands and have them repeat after me. When we got to the part about "left, right, left," I would say, "We look," and then point left, right, and left as they would say it. I would do it three times with all of my body, energy, and exuberance. They were fired up. The morale and the commitment to excellence was so high during that peak season that my business center, which was once the worst in the free world, was now leading our division in production during the peak season.

Not only did we produce a lot of revenue, we also reduced the company's burden and increased the profitability on top of it to the tune of 10 plus million dollars in cost savings. What can clear expectations and taking of responsibility do for a business unit that is worst in the free world? It can turn it into a leader and a model unit – a highly exceptional unit.

Chapter 8
Using the Keys 2.0

My last application example is about a promising company going into its fifth year at the time of this writing that I have been able to provide coaching and training to. Unlike Target and UPS, there is little familiarity you have with this company and it therefore warrants me to give a little bit of background about it.

This company found itself in a position where going into its fourth year, there had to be a severing of partnership between owners. This company found itself in a place of tremendous organizational change and having a need for exceptional change management.

What is necessary to share about the background of this company is that three months into the next year, which was also three months into the new ownership dynamic, this company was doing good but yet in a difficult place because it needed some unique TLC. The trajectory that the company could and should follow was set by the parting of ways by the partners but the company was still void of critical elements to solidify the preferred dynamics of the company.

When I got involved and began to assist in streamlining and focusing efforts, there began to be the ability to achieve more with less and to bring to the surface the company DNA. Interestingly, the quality-of-life increased dramatically (work days became shorter), the earning potential increased equally even without the same volume of business.

At the point where there was a declaration made to the entire team and company that the company was no longer in recovery mode from the change in ownership, unbelievable things began to happen. The unbelievable began to happen because at that point was the adoption of a specific mentality to guide interactions with customers and the introduction of the two keys for highly exceptional teams – expectation and responsibility.

These two keys were documented and presented as the core perspective of everything that is done through the company. That is, whether dealing with colleagues, customers, or vendors and suppliers, the expectation for the engagement with these would often and always guide responsibility. Regardless of what they are called upon to do or who they are called to engage, what would be necessary is for them to understand clearly what is expected to be delivered upon and then to appropriately use their ability and respond with excellence.

Let me give you a look into two proofs. The first is about one of the professionals who was experiencing challenges in making the transition within the scope of a specific job type. This professional was experiencing tremendous, I mean tremendous, challenge with their specific job type.

It was not clear from them or from management what the issue was, and it was creating serious frustrations. Conversation was taking place on a weekly bases over the course of a few months. Mistakes were becoming repetitive related to that job type. It was very clear that there was an issue but there was a difficulty it getting to the root of this issue.

There was a moment where I was brought into the picture to help engage this particular professional. After listening to the professional and their supervisor discuss the matter at hand, I went to the whiteboard and listed four bullet points. I'm not going to go into the bullet points in-depth. I simply want to give you a sense of what took place.

There were four bullet points given and each bullet point represented a job type. What we were able to do was paint a picture about what each job type involved and therefore what each job type required of the professional in time and engagement.

Needless to say, the professional saw that each job type had a different level of commitment that was required, which meant that the commitment he was giving to the job type in question was more than was required or expected. Did you hear that? Expected. You heard right; the professional realized that he did not understand the expectation.

As a matter of fact, you should have seen the excitement he had when he saw that he was putting the wrong amount of time and effort into the job type he was challenged by than what was expected. He went out that very same day, applied what he learned and was now clear on the expectation, and made a 180° turn around in how he engaged his responsibility on that job type.

Take notice of something though. This professional said prior to the awareness of this expectation that he would not change the way he was approaching the job type in question. Why did he change? It was because he had an inherent desire to take responsibility or respond with his ability to do what was consistent with what would bring the greatest value.

The reason the professional was responding with his ability inappropriately to the specific job type was because he thought the expectation was consistent with how he was responding with his ability. Once he became clear about the expectation for that job type and considered it related to the responsibility he already had, there was no way he could behave inappropriately without violating his responsibility and the expectations.

The second proof is related to a shift in mindset. Another professional was wanting to grow in their customer engagement to influence better sales interactions. There was an opportunity to have some conversations with him over a period of time and the subject of expectation and responsibility in the customer engagement emerged.

What was painted for this professional was a picture of the reality that every customer has an expectation that arises with their problem but the customer is limited in their responsibility which is why there is an opportunity for him to be standing before the customer. The customer is looking to him as one who is able to take responsibility and deliver upon an expectation. What expectation is that though?

Well, every customer has an expectation that they approach a company with. That ultimate expectation is for the thing that they cannot do themselves to get done. So, it's imperative that the person who interfaces with the customer seek to understand with great clarity the customer's expectation. This is necessary so that when the professional, regardless of their environment, then seeks to provide solutions for the customer, they're able to effectively respond with their ability committed to a clear expectation that will leave the customer exceptionally satisfied.

This professional also was excited about this awareness and immediately began to use the two keys. Not only did it change the dynamics of his customer engagement and sales results, it transformed him in such a way that he desired to grow and make changes in order to be a better person for himself more than for customers. His words to me were, "There are things about me that I am seeing that I had not seen before…and because of you, I am committed to expanding my communication ability."

What happened to both of these professionals for this young company and within the scope of the more established companies above? The two keys enabled all the people to see how exceptional they could be and empowered them to pursue it. You see, these two keys transform, inspire, and enrich individuals in a way that has a reciprocal effect on teams that is compounded.

When you get down to the nuts and bolts of it, the truth of the matter is that a highly exceptional team is nothing more than a combination of highly exceptional people who have a commitment and clarity of expectation and responsibility. It may sound simple or cheesy but I promise you this is more critical than you could have ever known.

The young company that I mentioned above can certainly testify about this. At the time of this writing, they have experienced a 25% growth from last year to this year and are in a position to where it could potentially be 30 to 40 before the year is out. Guess what? It's because of a value for an appropriate commitment and clarity of expectation and responsibility.

Chapter 9
Rise & Fall

In this short volume of a book, we have talked about some very meaty matters. I want to sum up this book with a quote from Dr. John C. Maxwell but first let me tell a quick story about him. Before I ever became a certified speaker, teacher, and coach of The John Maxwell Team, Dr. Maxwell was my leadership teacher or better yet my leadership professor. It was not in the classroom but through his books.

I remember walking into the book store at 19 years old and seeing *The Maxwell Leadership Bible* and thinking that he had passed away. How interesting it was that later on down the line I learned he had not passed away but was doing extremely well, speaking publicly, and still writing books. I always get a kick out of that story, but I digress.

One of the major ideas about leadership that Dr. Maxwell has boasted for years is that, "Everything rises and falls on leadership." When I first heard those words, they were like music my to ears and honey in my mouth. Today they are like lifeblood to me because I have seen how true they are regardless of how true he said they were.

I have seen for myself how the violation of the leadership laws he teaches have extreme effects of the advancement of problems and chaos. The same is the case here with these two keys; when not regarded or respected, success and achievement are nothing but a dream.

You see when you go back and look at the examples that I gave, you will find that at the core of the rise to excellence or the fall to issue and problem was leadership. What I mean is that it was someone who had a position of influence who was able to impact the awareness that affected the results. My point in bringing this up is to say with absolute certainty that if there is a void in the area of expectation and responsibility it is at the level of leadership.

No sugar coating here folks. No excusing those who depend on leadership. No giving a pass to anyone. What is to be understood is that a tree cannot grow and produce fruit without there first being a seed sown.

Someone has to sow the seed before someone can prune the tree. Someone has to sow the seed before fruit can grow that can be picked by someone else. Someone has to sow the seed before the seeds of the fruit that are picked can produce more trees from other seeds sown. The point is that for expectation and responsibility to produce abundant fruit in the form of highly exceptional results, people and teams, it has to start with somebody – a leader – making them clear.

Let's think back on the Bible story mentioned earlier. The master gave to his servants according to their ability. Though we don't see it specifically stated, we are able to observe later in the engagement surrounding the settling of accounts that the expectations were made very clear from the master to the servants.

We find that two of the servants were clear on the expectation and therefore responded with their ability diligently and expeditiously. However, we saw that with the same expectations and responsibility to deliver on those expectations, one servant did not respond with his ability appropriately.

From a statistical perspective this leader was proven to have been exceptional in his leadership because he had two thirds of his team to produce according to what was expected. This metric gives the sense that not everybody will measure up even when leaders do their part, and that there can be significant value and benefit without 100% effort. Still though, everything rises and falls on leadership. That means that leadership is not just the responsibility of the initiating leader. It is also the responsibility of subordinate leaders.

The effect of leadership is that it goes from one leader down to another leader and to another leader and to another leader. The point is that every individual person has a sphere of leadership or influence. Dr. Maxwell often teaches that "the true measure of leadership is influence– nothing more, nothing less." So, when the initiating leader engages their expectation and responsibility and then makes clear the expectation and responsibility for those who depend on them, it commissions the subordinate leaders to respond with their leadership ability and deliver upon the expectations within the scope of their environment and role.

Listen, there is so much more that can be said about all of the different things discussed in this book. The point is not to say a whole lot. The point is to say a little with great impact to inspire mindset and enrich life pursuit of the greatest value. The point is to stimulate thought and subsequent action. The point is to stress that when there is a clarity of what is expected, it is less likely for ability to be responded with inconsistent with that ability.

I end with this. When I was in high school, I quit four sports including cross-country which I mentioned earlier. Mind you I was skilled at all of these sports. Looking back, I should have chosen the sports that I was most able to excel at and then give my full attention and commitment to those to be my best, but I didn't have that awareness. That expectation was not set for me. If I am honest though, I can blame no one but myself.

If I had set the expectation for myself to give my best effort in every sport I committed to, I would have never quit. I would have had a commitment to exhaust all of my ability into whatever sport for the time that it was required of me.

Unfortunately, I found myself to be in the mindset of that one servant who took what was given to him by his master and buried it. Not only did I bury it, I had the gall to dig it up and present it to him as if I was doing him a favor. The truth was that I was operating out of limited beliefs and mediocrity, and therefore not being the highly exceptional person I was created to be.

I believe that if we take these two keys in conjunction with any law, concept, strategy, or anything like these, we will not only be highly exceptional people or highly exceptional teams, we will be highly exceptional leaders creating legacies that impact generations far beyond our reach. Not only will we create organizations, endeavors, and cities that can be around for hundreds of years, but we will be able to create a framework that influences a certain mindset that can reproduce excellent morale and value beyond the measure of any price point.

I think that we lack the economic strength globally that we can truly have because of not clearly making known expectation and responsibility as well as holding one another lovingly accountable to these two keys. I think in the future I may actually talk about love in business, but for now I just want to state that at the heart of clear expectations and taking of responsibility is a love for the individuals who make up a team.

I don't mean the emotional love in its romantic sense or love in the sense of relationship with immediate relatives. I mean love in the sense of commitment and devotion to those who are committed to the same goals, desires, dreams, and impact.

I think that if we get this right, greatness like we have never seen before will emerge and shift the trajectory of our current landscape of life as well as the future prospects in a highly exceptional manner.

So I say...

Ensure and commit to clear expectations. Take full responsibility. Influence highly exceptional teams.

#TheExtraMILEwithLeo

I'm a giver and encourager, so allow me to add value to your growth and development in a positive way.

Go to YouTube and search #TheExtraMILEwithLeo.
Subscribe to my channel and follow me.
Content is released weekly.
Do check out past episodes.
Be sure to tune in to be inspired and enriched!

Make A Difference

My wife and I volunteer with a non-profit called

Have your heard of Apartment Life? If you haven't, you can learn about it at apartmentlife.org.

I am firm believer that when there are ways in which to contribute and support endeavors that help in the advancement of others, awareness about such is of benefit because you never know who might also desire to contribute.

So, would you be open to contributing to a worthy tax-deductible cause and endeavor? Yes!

Here's an exciting cause and endeavor to contribute to.

So, if the difference that Apartment Life is making is exciting to you, I invite you to also make a difference with a financial contribution as great as your excitement.

Make your financial contribution at
tinyurl.com/contribute-2-apartmentlife.

#BeTheRealYou

Let me ask you some quick questions...

Do you have potential?
(You answer is likely, Yes)

Do you know the types of potential you possess?
(Note: There are only 2)

Do you know the 3 elements of converting your potential?

Do you know the 15 laws that enable you to tap into your potential?

If you answered, No, to any 1 of these questions,

"You don't know who you are yet!"

But you can with the
#BeTheRealYou E-Course

To preview and purchase the E-Course,
go to
www.udemy.com/be-the-real-you

Book Leo

Leo is available for keynotes, seminars, and trainings to inspire your team and influence transformational results.

To inquire about inviting Leo to speak at next your event,
go to
www.team3L.com/book-leo

www.ingramcontent.com/pod-product-compliance
Lightning Source LLC
Chambersburg PA
CBHW021509210526
45463CB00002B/961